QUEENS
THROUGH TIME

RICHARD PANCHYK

AMERICA
THROUGH TIME®
ADDING COLOR TO AMERICAN HISTORY

America Through Time is an imprint of Fonthill Media LLC
www.through-time.com
office@through-time.com

Published by Arcadia Publishing by arrangement with Fonthill Media LLC
For all general information, please contact Arcadia Publishing:
Telephone: 843-853-2070
Fax: 843-853-0044
E-mail: sales@arcadiapublishing.com
For customer service and orders:
Toll-Free 1-888-313-2665

www.arcadiapublishing.com

First published 2022

Copyright © Richard Panchyk 2022

ISBN 978-1-63499-432-3

Typeset in Mrs Eaves XL Serif Narrow
Printed and bound in England

Acknowledgments

Thanks to Lizzy for her company on many a Queens adventure for this and other Queens books. Thanks to Kena Smith for her support and help, and thanks to Kimberly Black for her feedback. Special thanks to the Queens Library for their enthusiasm for all my Queens titles. And a special shout out to my history-packed hometown of Elmhurst for inspiring my love of all things Queens!

Credits

All images courtesy of the author except as noted below:

National Archives: page 8 (top), page 12, page 17 (top), page 27 (bottom), page 36, page 40 (top), page 43 (top), page 45 (top), page 49 (top), page 52, page 53 (top), page 56 (top), page 57 (top), page 58 (top), page 59 (top), page 60 (top), page 61 (top), page 62, page 65 (bottom), page 66 (bottom), page 67 (top), page 68 (top).

Library of Congress: page 9 (bottom), page 10 (top), page 11 (top), page 25 (top), page 32, page 33 (top), page 35 (top), page 46 (top), page 47, page 48 (top), page 51 (bottom), page 54, page 57 (bottom), page 58 (bottom), page 63 (top), page 80 (top), page 92 (top).

USGS: page 91 (bottom).

INTRODUCTION

Originally a vast expanse of land that comprised today's Queens and Nassau Counties, early Queens consisted of a core handful of original 17th century settlements such as Newtown, Flushing, Jamaica, and Hempstead. The two main groups that founded early Queens towns were the Dutch and the English; even after the permanent English takeover of the colony in 1674, the Dutch presence remained so pronounced for decades after, such that many place names in Queens are Dutch in origin, including Flushing, which was originally called Vlissingen after a city in the Netherlands.

Queens was just a stone's throw away from New York City (which then consisted solely of Manhattan) but for hundreds of years it took a ferry ride to get there as no bridges or tunnels crossed the water. Queens led a fully separate existence from the city, and was along with Brooklyn, considered to be "Long Island."

Though it was not yet part of New York City, Colonial era Queens had moments of great historical significance. For example, the Flushing Remonstrance of 1657 was one of the important documents in the fight for religious freedom. Queens is also the site of perhaps the only building still standing in the United States where a future English monarch worshiped – the St. James Church in Elmhurst (then Newtown), where the future King William IV was stationed when he was in the British Navy as a teenager. The town of Newtown also gave birth to what was for a time the most famous apple in the world, the Newtown Pippin variety, which was a mutation that grew on an orchard belonging to the Moore family. This apple was immediately recognized for its potential and cultivated. Word spread quickly and the Newtown Pippin was favored by Benjamin Franklin and Thomas Jefferson and to this day is known for its intense, sweet-tart flavor. one of the last of the surviving 18th century Newtown pippin trees (150 years old) was photographed in 1902 in Elmhurst (see photo on page X). Though now grown elsewhere, the Newtown Pippin is still to this day a prized (if uncommon) variety of apple.

During the Revolution, Queens, like New York City, was occupied by the British. After the war, it continued to grow, albeit much more slowly than Manhattan, which was expanding rapidly. Between 1770 and 1810, Queens grew from 11,000 to 19,000 people while Manhattan surged from about 20,000 to 96,000 people. By the mid-nineteenth century, Queens contained an eclectic mixture of farmland, residential, commercial, and industrial areas. Because there was still much land available for development, several large cemeteries were opened in Queens to handle the burial needs of a growing Manhattan.

Everything changed with the creation of modern New York City in 1898. Eastern Queens separated and soon became Nassau County, while western Queens was annexed into New York City (along with Brooklyn, Staten Island, and the Bronx), which had previously consisted solely of Manhattan.

In the early years of the 20th century, the first bridge was built across the East River, and the first tunnels were dug under the river to carry the Long Island Rail Road and New York City subways. Queens had quickly changed from a bucolic, distant-seeming place that could only be reached by boat to a thriving part of the city, from whence you could reach Manhattan within 30 minutes from many locations. The last of the farmland was soon developed as commuting to work in Manhattan was now a viable option and residential developments blossomed throughout the borough. As Queens quickened, the Rockaways, which had been a vacation getaway, became more of a residential area.

As the decades passed, Queens continued to grow. Highways such as the Grand Central Parkway and Long Island Expressway were constructed, further quickening life. Queens also became New York City's airport hub, with numerous smaller airfields serving as predecessors to today's remaining big two – LaGuardia and JFK airports. Between 1900 and 1950, the population of Queens grew by a factor of 10, from about 150,000 to 1.5 million! Though it was part of New York City, it still retained a very strong sense of place – being from Queens was a source of pride for its residents.

Queens has also hosted two World's Fairs (1939 and 1964) and is home to the New York Mets (and formerly the New York Jets). The Mets' original home, Shea Stadium, will be forever famous for the Beatles concert that took place there in 1965, at the height of Beatlemania. Concerts sometimes still take place at the Mets' current home, Citi Field, as well as at the Forest Hills Tennis Stadium, which has seen its share of musical events (and tennis matches) over the years. The US Open Tennis Championship was originally played at Forest Hills, and is now held at the USTA Billie Jean King National Tennis Center across from Citi Field in Flushing.

The city's two airports are located in Queens, both the descendants and survivors of what used to be several airfields in the borough. Aviation has played an important part in Queens history and development, going back to the days when naval aviators flew seaplanes from the Rockaways in 1919 on a mission to become the first to cross the Atlantic.

With all the changes of the 20th century came much growth, yet the settlements within Queens still managed to retain their own distinct identities and history. There are still some 17th and 18th century buildings scattered throughout Queens, along with scores of 19th century structures. As time passes, countless thousands of Queens homes are reaching the century mark; many of the borough's neighborhoods are filled with single-family or multi-family attached homes that were built between 1900 and 1940. To this day, each neighborhood has a very unique culture, flavor, and identity (for example, when you address an envelope to Queens, you don't write Queens, NY 11373, you write Elmhurst, NY

11373, unlike the other boroughs). The large borough's widely varying topography helps in this regard – from the hilly ridge running through central Queens (the point of furthest expansion of the glaciers during the last Ice Age) to the beachfront streets of the Rockaways to the untouched colonial-era forest of giant trees in Alley Pond Park, there is great variety in the terrain depending on where in Queens you happen to be. Queens locales are packed with history and a well-defined sense of place. Yet in addition to that ever-present sense of community, Queens itself has a strong sense of identity. To be from Queens means something very distinct and unique, no matter how large and varied the borough actually is. Whether Astoria or Glen Oaks, Bayside or Belle Harbor, Queens is a special place.

In this book, which I have arranged geographically by location in a roughly west to east fashion, you will see some examples of how drastically things have changed over the years, and other examples of how much things have remained that same. Queens' growth has resulted in much destruction and renewal, but thankfully also in much preservation and celebration of the past.

A note about postcards: Some of the vintage images in this book are from old postcards. In the early 20th century, the subject matter of postcards was surprisingly mundane as compared with what we see today. Tree-lined streets, high schools, libraries, churches, seemingly anything and everything was postcard-worthy. In those days, time and space had a very different meaning than in today's fast-paced and easily reachable world. Before subways and buses criss-crossed Queens, before automobiles became commonplace, a trip to the Rockaways, or Flushing, or Jamaica was an adventure that could take several hours. Seemingly ordinary places in Queens were rather exotic and interesting because many people who lived in Brooklyn, Manhattan, the Bronx, Staten Island, Long Island, New Jersey, and Connecticut (for example) had never been there. Getting a card from your friend visiting Forest Hills was exciting. The turn of the 20th century was also a period of great growth in New York City, so postcards often depicted the latest "wonders" in construction, such as new government buildings or residential developments. As Queens turned from farmland to suburbs, postcards documented that change, and so are very useful tools in a book such as this one.

Now known as the RFK (Robert F. Kennedy) Bridge, the Triborough Bridge was descriptively named for the fact that it connects three boroughs: Queens, Manhattan, and the Bronx. Opened in 1936, the bridge is described by the MTA as "the authority's flagship bridge." The suspension bridge that everyone thinks of is actually only a part of the overall bridge facility, which includes viaducts/approaches, a truss bridge, and a vertical lift bridge. The evening of its opening, thousands of spectators took the bridge to Randalls Island to watch athlete Jesse Owens qualify for the 1936 Olympics. At top is the Queens approach as seen in 1943 and at bottom a 2017 photo of the bridge seen from the streets of from Astoria.

The Queensboro Bridge (aka the 59th Street Bridge and the Edward I. Koch Bridge, after the former mayor of New York City) was built in 1909 and provided the first bridge connection between Manhattan and Queens. At top, a c1910s image of the Queensboro bridge with Manhattan in the foreground, Roosevelt Island in the middle (then known as Blackwell's Island), and Queens in the background. At bottom, the bridge seen in a 1978 photo looking toward Roosevelt Island in the foreground and Queens in the background.

A tale of two Queens mansions. At top, the Bodine mansion at 43-16 Vernon Boulevard in Long Island City as seen just before its demolition in 1966. At bottom, the Steinway mansion on 41st Street in Astoria. The Steinway company expanded its operations to a 400-acre plot of land in Astoria in the 1870s. The family bought an 1858 mansion on a bluff that once offered pleasant views of the waterfront. Built in 1858, the twenty-six-room house (seen in 2017) had belonged to Benjamin Pike, Jr., an optician.

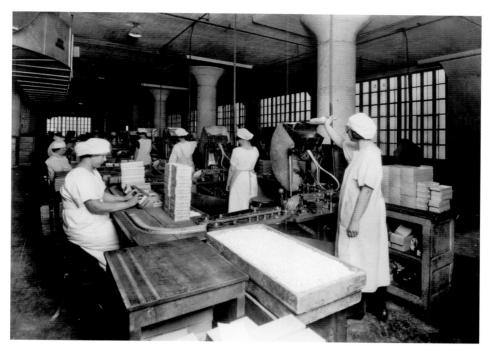

Long Island City was one of New York's biggest industrial areas and was home to many important manufacturers in the first half of the twentieth century. The American Chicle Company, manufacturer of the famous Chiclets brand gum, was located at 30-30 Thomson Avenue in Long Island City. At top, the employees work in the Chiclet packing department at the Queens plant in 1923. At bottom, the lobby courtyard of 30-30 Thomson Avenue building in 2018.

At top, a World War I defense plant manufacturing gas masks needed for the war effort in Long Island City, *circa* 1917/18. Note boxes on the conveyor belts at left and masks on the tables at right. At bottom, the first troops return home arriving at Long Island City in December 1918 just after the Armistice.

Rails on Queens streets used to be a common sight throughout Queens, but they are long gone now. At top is a trolley barn in Maspeth. At bottom, the remains of train tracks in Long Island City for rail spurs that used to serve the many industrial buildings in the area.

There are about 15,000 fire call boxes throughout New York City. Many of them are very old, dating to 1910s, 20s, or 30s. A lot of them are in rough condition but dozens have been restored by a security guard from Queens named John Colgan, who has repainted them bright shades of red and gold. At left, an unrestored call box photographed in 2018, and below, a restored one photographed in Woodside in 2017.

Like many Queens communities, Maspeth experienced growth and development during the early to mid-twentieth century. After Queens became part of New York City, much of the borough transitioned from farmland to residential, commercial, and industrial neighborhoods. At top, Maspeth homes on a residential street *circa* late 1920s (the sender of the postcard marked his own home with an X), and at bottom, two women sit on a tree stump in Maspeth *c*1930s. Inset: A Maspeth street off Grand Avenue in 2022.

The forty-four-room Grand Motor Inn, located on Grand Avenue in Maspeth, is a survivor from another era. Built in 1931, it was purchased in 2017 for $7.5 million, and as of 2022 was still in operation. Motor Inns were popular in the 1940s-1970s era. At top, *c*1960s; at bottom in 2022.

In the days when school properties still contained undeveloped land, Queens schoolkids were taught farming. At top, kids from PS 88 in Ridgewood are farming a 1-½ acre "War Garden" during the summer of 1918 under the supervision of their principal. At bottom, kids from PS 102 in Elmhurst prepare the soil for crops in the 1920s.

The old Moore homestead on Broadway in Elmhurst was built in the 1660s and demolished in 1929 due to construction on the IND subway line. It was home to the family whose branches included the famous Christmas poem author, Clement Clarke Moore, and the Episcopal bishop, Benjamin Moore, who gave the last rites to Alexander Hamilton after the fatal duel. The spot today is home to the Moore Homestead Playground, seen below in 2017. Though local lore has Clement Clarke Moore writing the poem in the house or living in it, his father was actually born about a half mile to the west, a site which is currently occupied by an apartment building (see inset).

The original St. James Church was built in what was then Newtown (now Elmhurst) in 1735. It remained standing (and is now one of the oldest buildings in New York) but was replaced by a new building across Broadway, built in 1848 and seen at top *circa* 1905. That building burned down in the 1970s and was replaced by the current church structure, seen below in 2020.

One of the country's earliest suburban experiments was the idea of Samuel Lord, department store owner of Lord & Taylor. Lord developed a parcel of land in what was then Newtown (now Elmhurst) and had four houses built upon it. These thirteen-room homes were designed to be desirable for the middle class, and convenient for a commute to Manhattan, as they were a short walk to the railroad station. The idea fizzled as the homes were divided into apartments. At top, an image of Clermont Terrance as it was called, around the turn of the twentieth century. At bottom, a staircase was among the last small remnants of one of the Lord houses (the last of which was demolished in 2006), seen in 2017.

Two vanished diners: The Georgia Diner was for decades a mainstay on the north side of Queens Boulevard in Elmhurst. Located in a highly desirable spot near major shopping centers, the property was bought by a developer for $14.25 million; a few years earlier the same developer had purchased part of the Georgia parking lot for $26.5 million. The diner closed in 2018 and was demolished. Inset: The author enjoys a last meal at the old Georgia Diner in 2018. It relocated to the south side of Queens Boulevard and merged with the Nevada Diner (formerly the Sage Diner). At bottom, the Goodfellas Diner at 56-26 Maspeth Avenue in Maspeth was so named for a famous scene from the iconic movie that was filmed there. This photo is from 2016; the diner burned down in 2018.

The Ascension Catholic School was built in the 1950s on 53rd Avenue (property extending to Grand Avenue) in Elmhurst to serve a growing population. An old house across the street was converted into a convent, seen at top in 1957 and at bottom in 2008.

Looking north from near Van Horn Street, down 55th Road in Elmhurst (then known as Homans Avenue), in 1922 when the one-family homes seen here had just been completed on the former property of the Bretonniere Farm, and at bottom, looking north along a street in the same neighborhood in 2010. The round Macy's building on Queens Boulevard is visible in the background. Many of the original row houses in the "Nassau Heights" section of Elmhurst have been modernized and expanded, with porches enclosed and extensions added in the rear.

The iconic, modernistic round Macy's building was constructed in the mid-1960s on Queens Boulevard in Elmhurst. Seen above in 1992 and below in 2018, the Macy's moved to what used to be the Queens Center Mall and a Target became the anchor store of what became itself a mini mall.

During the early days of the Revolution, the British had control of Queens. General William Howe, commander of the British forces in America, made his headquarters in Newtown, at the Renne farmhouse, located just off what is now the south side of Queens Boulevard at 56th Street. The historic house was demolished in 1937. At top, an eighteenth-century image of General Howe. At bottom, the former site of the Renne House as it appeared in 2015, with no trace of the history that was once there.

The Elmwood Theater in Elmhurst was built as the Queensboro Theater in 1928 just as the industry was transitioning to talkies, and for many decades served the community. The theater closed in 2002 and the building was converted into the Rock Church. At top, the Elmwood Theater in 1995. At bottom, a 1996 flyer for a historical program about the Elmwood Theater on the corner of Queens Boulevard and 57th Street in Elmhurst.

HONORABLE JOHN SABINI CITY COUNCIL MEMBER

CENTRAL QUEENS HISTORICAL ASSOCIATION

QUEENS BOROUGH PUBLIC LIBRARY

Invites _you_ to the Fiftieth Anniversary of the naming of the Elmwood Movie Theatre

AIR CONDITIONED   **FREE ADMISSION**

THURSDAY, SEPTEMBER 5, 1996 AT 7:30 P.M.
LOCATED AT 57-02 HOFFMAN DRIVE
● _DISCUSSION OF THE ARCHITECTURE AND HISTORY OF THE ELMWOOD_●
● _INTERACTION BETWEEN THE THEATRE AND COMMUNITY EXAMINED_●
● _FUTURE OF THE ELMWOOD LOOKED AT_ ●
● _SHOWING OF A QUALITY PERIOD FILM_ ●

HOST: COUNCILMEMBER JOHN SABINI

FOR FURTHER INFORMATION,
CALL ELLEN RAFFAELE AT (718) 507-3688 OR JEFF GOTTLIEB AT (718) 793-2255

THE CHUTES, NORTH BEACH.

Spent aug. 24 1905 here with mary, florence and myself. E.J.

Before one of New York's two major airports was built in Flushing, the North Beach amusement park occupied the site. Opened in 1886, the complex was the idea of piano manufacturer William Steinway and included a beach, a swimming pool, theaters, picnic grounds, pavilions, and a Ferris Wheel. Water pollution and changing times led to a decrease in its popularity by the 1920s. At top, the North Beach water chutes as seen in 1905. At bottom, the future LaGuardia Airport under construction in 1939. This view looks north.

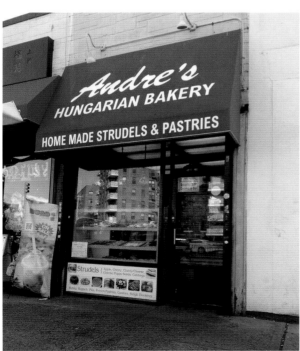

Queens used to be home to numerous bakeries, but as supermarkets grew in size and popularity and had their own bakery departments, and big box stores proliferated and offered their own cheap baked goods, the number of bakeries in Queens dwindled. At top, the longtime Middle Village favorite Bauer's Bake Shop on Dry Harbor Road in 2010 (since closed) and at bottom, Andre's Hungarian Bakery on Queens Boulevard in Rego Park in 2018 (still open as of 2022).

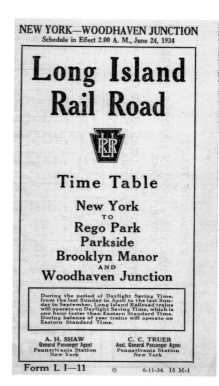

Long Island Rail Road used to offer service to the Rockaways, and Rego Park had a station on that line. The station opened in 1928 but closed in 1962 when the Rockaway Line was shut down for good. At top is a 1934 train schedule for the Rockaway Line and at bottom, the abandoned tracks near Metropolitan Avenue in Forest Hills.

A rare microburst (downburst from a thunderstorm) struck Forest Hills on September 16, 2010, devastating the trees of MacDonald Park (just off Queens Boulevard) with 125 mph winds, tearing off large limbs and uprooting huge trees. The photograph at top was taken at the park by the author on September 25, 2010; at bottom, the park in 2022. Note the young trees that had been recently planted.

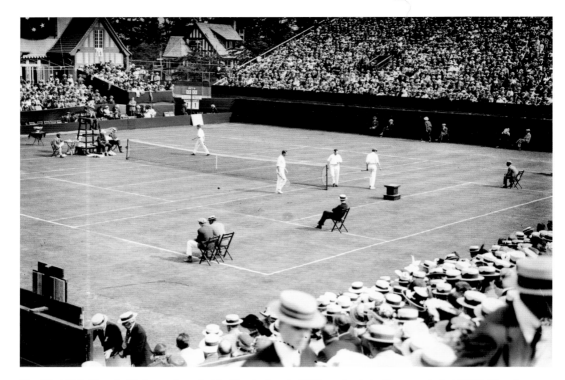

The West Side Tennis Club was founded in Manhattan in 1892, and originally operated at 238th Street. Looking for more room, they relocated to a spacious site in Forest Hills in 1914 (just west of the train station), where by 1915, the precursor to the U.S. Open was held every year. At top, changing courts at the Davis Cup championships on August 14, 1914; the Davis Cup can be seen on the table at left. At bottom, a doubles championship match at Forest Hills on August 29, 1916.

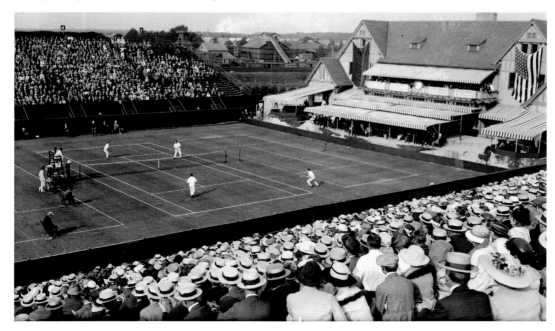

In 1923, Forest Hills stadium was built on the site. At top, the women's championship match at the newly built stadium in 1924 Forest Hills and at bottom, Andre Agassi plays in the Shearson-Lehman Tournament of Champions at the stadium in May 1987. The stadium hosts concerts by some of the biggest names in music. Over the years, acts such as Paul Simon, Ed Sheeran, Genesis, the Monkees, and Tom Petty and the Heartbreakers have appeared at Forest Hills.

31-17

At top, Gown Street (now Continental Avenue) in Forest Hills around the turn of the 20th century. At bottom: The Tudor-style Forest Hills Inn is part of the historic Forest Hills Gardens development that was built c1909/10. With 150 rooms and a location directly across from the railroad station, the Inn was a home to both visitors and permanent residents. In 1967, it was converted into a residential building. For a time in the 1970s and 1980s, its restaurant was converted to a Beefsteak Charlie's.

The Forest Hills train station was built in 1906 as part of the overall historic Tudor-style Station Square complex that includes the Forest Hills Inn building. When completed, the subway system had not yet reached the area, so the station was a valuable improvement to Queens transportation. At top, the pedestrian bridge and wall at the station in 1941. At bottom, the station in 2022.

Two aerials of Flushing taken just three years apart show the dramatic improvements made at the site of the 1939 World's Fair, converting it from a lifeless refuse dump into a magical place that would be visited by millions of people. At top, an aerial view of the site on November 30, 1936, and at bottom, development is well under way on August 23, 1938. Almost all of the 1939-40 World's Fair was demolished shortly after the fair ended. Steel was reused for the war effort. The main survivor was the New York City Pavilion building, which was intended to be permanent. For a few years in the late 1940s, it was home to the General Assembly of the United Nations. It was reused during the 1964 World's Fair and later housed the Queens Museum.

While the 1939 World's Fair did have a focus on the future and included many interesting modernistic displays, such as television (which was introduced to the American public at the '39 Fair), there was also some nostalgia. Seen above is the New England section of the Court of States, with a celebration of the area's seafaring heritage. At bottom, an artist's rendering of the Johnson Wax Pavilion at the '64 Fair, which included a 30-foot-thick gold disc containing a theater, suspended 24 feet above the ground.

New York World's Fair 1939

Both the 1939 and 1964 World's Fairs were filled with futuristic buildings and exhibits. The 1964 Fair had a decidedly "Space Age" flavor to it, with many of the buildings having a very Jetsons feel to them. At top, the Maritime Building at the 1939 Fair (with a main entrance flanked by twin ship prows) and at bottom, the General Motors Futurama Building at the 1964 Fair. The latter featured a 110-foot-high sloping canopy over the entrance.

Colors and lights were important at both World's Fairs. At top, Food Building Number Three at the 1939 Fair, with colorful light beams in the background. At bottom, the Tower of Light at the 1964 Fair. Its description reads: "The world's most powerful searchlight beam rises from the center of this unusual building. The exterior walls consist of 600 aluminum prisms in a unique pattern."

Both World's Fairs featured a giant globe as a centerpiece. At the 1939 Fair it was called the Perisphere (180 feet in diameter) and was accompanied by a 610-foot-high tower called the Trylon. At the 1964 Fair it was called the Unisphere (120 feet in diameter), only this time it was just a steel sculptural figure, not a building like in 1939. The Unisphere was made to be permanent, a gift to the city of New York, and was dedicated to "Peace and Understanding." Another of the highlights of the 1964 Fair was the New York State Pavilion, seen at bottom in 2018. The structure, easily visible to thousands daily from the Long Island Expressway, had fallen into neglect. A restoration began in 2019.

A 1961 artist's rendering of the Main Mall of the 1964 World's Fair, featuring the Unisphere. At bottom, the Unisphere as seen in 2017. The Unisphere is one of the largest of the remaining 1964 World's Fair structures and is a focal point of Flushing Meadows Corona Park.

After the Brooklyn Dodgers and the New York Giants left the city in the late 1950s, National League baseball fans were in mourning. The debut of the New York Mets in 1962 brought another Major League back to the city. In their first two seasons, the Mets played at the old home of the Giants, the Polo Grounds. Their new home, Shea Stadium in Flushing, was finished in 1964. At top, a boy touches home plate of a model of Shea Stadium, c1963. At bottom, an artist's rendering of the stadium, 1963.

Besides hosting the Mets (and Jets until 1983) Shea Stadium has hosted many concerts and special events, including the Beatles in 1964. At top, a packed Shea Stadium in 1965, and at bottom, a packed Shea Stadium welcomes Pope John Paul II on his visit to New York in 1979.

2009, the National League's New York Mets moved from Shea Stadium, their Flushing home since 1964, to a new stadium built in what was previously the Shea parking lot. Fans during the 2008 season got to see glimpses of the new Citi Field during the last games at Shea. Citi Field opened March 29, 2009. At top, the view from a game at Shea on August 11, 2008, and at bottom, Citi Field on June 25, 2021.

Though convenient to both a NYC subway stop and a Long Island Rail Road station, parking has always been essential for New York Mets fans arriving from neighborhoods without subway service or those fans living outside the city. Seen here are the Shea Stadium and Citi Field Parking lots, in 1973 and 2021.

The Cedar Grove cemetery in Flushing was just twelve years old when the top image was captured in 1905. The roadway infrastructure looks brand new. At bottom, the cemetery as seen in 2020 from one of the dead-end streets off of Main Street. Located just east of the Van Wyck Expressway and near John Bowne High School, the non-sectarian cemetery was founded in 1893 and has about 36,000 interments.

The Bowne House in Flushing (1661) is not only one of the oldest structures in New York State, it is also one of the most historic. Built by John Bowne, an Englishman living in the then Dutch colony of New Netherlands, it was the site of a Quaker meeting that caused Bowne's arrest and deportation to Holland. Bowne appealed and won, and was able to return to Flushing. His fight for religious freedom was an important step in establishing freedom. The Bowne House has been a museum since 1947, but was a local landmark long before that. At top, the house in a *c*1860 stereoscopic view labeled on the back "Old Daddy Bowne's House," and at bottom as photographed in 1936.

The Quaker, aka Friends Meeting House, on Northern Boulevard in Flushing dates to 1694, making it one of the oldest buildings in New York State, and the oldest house of worship in continuous use. At top seen in a 1930s photograph, the building is overrun by ivy. Below, the historic structure as it appeared in 2021 looks more friendly.

Though the subway system covers much of Queens, its residents would be lost without the convenience of the extensive network of buses, which stop along all the major roads and transport people to every corner of the borough. At top, an express bus on Queens Boulevard in 1973, and at bottom, a bus in Flushing. The nineteenth-century Flushing Town Hall building is in the background.

Opposite page: The beautiful Flushing Courthouse, aka Town Hall, was built in 1862 on Northern Boulevard in Flushing. The building is now a multi-disciplinary arts center with a 308-seat theater, gallery, garden, classroom, and rehearsal space. Concerts are held there, and the space is also available for renting for events. At top, the building *circa* 1910 and at bottom in 2021.

As one of the oldest settlements in Queens, downtown Flushing has been a hub for commercial activity for hundreds of years. What exactly that activity looked like has changed drastically over the years, as evidenced by the image of Main Street at top *c*1906, showing quaint wood frame buildings and trolley tracks, and the 2018 image of Main Street at bottom, featuring mainly businesses reflecting the ethnic diversity that is Queens.

At top, the Wake-Up America/Lexington Day/Patriot's Day celebration on Fifth Avenue in Manhattan, April 19, 1917, including a float from Flushing High School, Queens, with banners reading: "Flushing High School," "Free Russia," and "Honor dearer than life." At bottom, an October 1942 image shows the High School Victory Corps at Flushing High School, a program offering war-related physical education activities. The government caption to this press photo read: "By the time these boys are old enough to join America's fighting forces they will be toughened to commando standards. Flushing High School, Queens, New York, has expanded its physical education activities to include the type of training made necessary by wartime."

During the World War I era, aircraft industry was booming in northern Queens. At top, twenty men sit atop the fuselage of a Model V plane at the L.W.F. Engineering Co. in College Point. At bottom, a 2016 photograph shows the former location of the Flushing Airport in College Point, which was in operation from 1927 until 1984.

In a strange turn of events, the purported logs from Abraham Lincoln's original birthplace cabin (he was born in 1809) in Kentucky wound up in storage in College Point after having been on display at various locations. At top, the logs being removed from storage in Queens to begin their long journey to Kentucky, where a memorial was to be constructed to coincide with the 100th anniversary of Lincoln's birth. At bottom, the reconstructed log cabin (at a smaller scale because it would not have fit full size inside the memorial) as photographed in 1940.

The Homestead Hotel - Kew Gardens, Long Island, N. Y.

In 1928, the Homestead Hotel was opened on Grenfell Street in Kew Gardens. This elegant building had 100 rooms and was advertised as being fifteen minutes from Times Square. The hotel contained a coffee shop, dining room, and cocktail lounge. It was eventually turned into the New Homestead, a retirement home. Above, the hotel as it appeared *circa* the early 1960s. At bottom, a 2018 photo of architectural details of the vintage Tudor-style building on Lefferts Boulevard in Kew Gardens that houses the Homestead Gourmet Shop, a German deli.

When this photograph was taken c1930s of the "Kew Gardens Loop" of crisscrossing highways, the area was not even fully developed yet. By the 1990s, the traffic congestion had become a problem. The New York State Department of Transportation initiated a massive Kew Gardens Interchange reconstruction program that led to widening of existing roadways and new ramps and bridges being built to modernize this busy interchange. At bottom, part of the newly reconstructed Kew Gardens Interchange in 2020.

The Bronx-Whitestone Bridge, along with the Throgs Neck Bridge, was an essential component in improving transportation around New York City. By connecting Queens to the Bronx, these bridges saved motorists from having to drive through Manhattan to get to points north and Connecticut. At top, the bridge in an aerial view from 1943, and at bottom the bridge in 1991.

The Whitestone Bridge Parkway as seen in 1940 and 1991. The bridge, along with its counterpart Throgs Neck Bridge, provided a much-needed direct connection between Queens and the Bronx, also allowing Long Island motorists to more easily get to points north and northeast of the city. Queens parkways back in the 1940s were far different from what they are today. The Whitestone Expressway underwent a major $100 million rehabilitation and widening in 2011.

Located on a 147-acre peninsula in the northern reaches of Queens, just east of the Throgs Neck Bridge, Fort Totten was for decades (starting in the Civil War era) an active army base. At top, a ceremony at Fort Totten in 1919 honoring a soldier with a distinguished service cross for bravery on the European front during the war that had ended the previous year. At bottom, Fort Totten today contains a New York City park, as well as FDNY and Army Reserve facilities. One of its buildings also houses the Bayside Historic Society.

The image at top shows businessmen signing application blanks to take the military training course at Fort Totten in 1918. Barracks buildings can be seen in the background. At bottom, one of those barracks, the Bachelors Officers' Quarters, seen abandoned and decaying in 2015. That building was restored and in 2019 became the home for the Center for the Women of New York.

Police Field Day - Jamaica, Long Island.
September 13, 1924. Photo by 14th Photo Section, Air Service, U. S. Army.

At top, Jamaica Field Day at the Jamaica racetrack in 1924 at what is now Rochdale Village east of Ozone Park. The Jamaica Race Course was demolished in 1960 to coincide with the opening of Aqueduct nearby, seen below in a vintage photograph.

Queens once hosted several smaller airports in various locations. With a growing aviation industry and the need for larger airports that were not so close to residential areas, the sites for LaGuardia and Kennedy airports made sense. At top, an early rendering of the planned Idlewild Airport in southern Queens, 1943. At bottom, President Barack Obama waves as he boards Air Force One at John F. Kennedy International Airport (so renamed after Kennedy's death in 1963) on July 30, 2012.

Before the railroad connected it to the mainland in 1880, the only way to get to this southern Queens island was by boat. With the rail connection and subsequent roadway bridge, Broad Channel became a popular vacation and fishing spot in the early twentieth century. By 1914, there were twenty-seven fishing clubs in Broad Channel. At top is a 1915 photo of the burgeoning community, and at bottom, a handsome red building in Broad Channel in 2017.

The Edgemere neighborhood in the Rockaways was at the turn of the twentieth century a popular vacation destination, but by the late 1960s, the neighborhood was in a steep decline and its buildings were crumbling. Its buildings were condemned and demolished as part of a New York City urban renewal program. Most of the streets remain deserted as of 2022, with street signs, fire hydrants, and some deteriorated asphalt the only signs that a residential neighborhood once stood there.

Jacob Riis Park on Rockaway Beach was created in 1912, one of the city's early beachfront parks. The Art Deco bathhouse was built in 1932 and is seen at top in a c1934 image. The park fell under the jurisdiction of the National Park Service in 1972 when Gateway National Recreation Area was created. At bottom, an image of the park from Nov. 7, 2012, just a week after Hurricane Sandy struck. It was being used as a temporary dumping ground for garbage from the hurricane. By that point, sanitation crews had collected nearly a quarter-million tons of debris.

Boardwalk showing the Oriental Hotel, Rockaway Beach, N. Y.

The Rockaways were immensely popular as a vacation and recreation spot during the early twentieth century. A little further west from the recreation spot, Rockaway Beach was also the site of a naval air station, from whence several seaplanes took off in May 1919, attempting to be the first craft to make it across the ocean. One of them, the NC-4, made it after numerous stops, becoming the first airplane to cross the Atlantic. Seen at bottom is the NC-1 in December 1918, capable of 1,200 horsepower and 80 miles per hour. It had a wingspan of 126 feet.

The FEMA photo at top was taken in the waterfront community of Belle Harbor in March 2013, several months after Hurricane Sandy, and shows demolition and cleanup work still ongoing to remove debris from houses destroyed by Hurricane Sandy. More than 5.5 million cubic yards of debris had been removed to that point. At bottom, the Belle Harbor beachfront in 2018.

Named after Samuel J. Tilden, governor of New York in the 1870s, Fort Tilden was built in 1917 at the western end of the Rockaway Peninsula. It continued to grow through the 1920s and 1930s, and by World War II, there were more than ninety buildings on the site. The base was abandoned in 1974 and turned over to the National Park Service, as part of the Gateway National Recreation Area. At top, the army conducts anti-aircraft tests in 1925, with three-inch rifles used against flying targets towed by planes at a height of 3,000-6,000 feet. At bottom, an abandoned artillery installation at Fort Tilden as seen in 2017.

Grace Church is a Victorian-era, Gothic-style gem that is located in the heart of downtown Jamaica on Jamaica Avenue. The current Episcopal church building was built in 1862 and is surrounded by a much older cemetery in which is buried the former governor of New York, John Alsop King, and his father, Rufus King, signer of the Constitution. Many of the gravestones in the cemetery date to the mid-to-late eighteenth century. At left, the church c1905, and at right in 2017.

King's Mansion, Kings Park, Jamaica, L. I.

Sitting on a property that is now a park, King Manor in Jamaica was built in 1750, and was purchased by U.S. Constitution signer Rufus King in 1805. The property was purchased by the Village of Jamaica in 1897; ownership was transferred to New York City in 1898. King Manor in Jamaica has survived several close calls that threatened to alter or destroy it over the years, including a plan to convert it into a public library and two fires. At top, King Manor *circa* 1910 and at bottom in 2017.

King Manor is unique in that not only has it survived mostly intact from the eighteenth century, but the large (considering its location in downtown Jamaica) parcel of land surrounding it has also survived. The park includes a playground and basketball courts. Another reason it is unique is its long tenure as a museum—it has been open to the public since 1900.

The Greek Revival-style Queens Borough Library at Jamaica seen in 1913, before Jamaica was the headquarters of the Central Library of Queens. The library is currently housed in a modern building on Merrick Boulevard/166th street just south of Hillside Avenue.

For well over 100 years, Jamaica Avenue (aka Fulton Street) has been an important commercial thoroughfare in Jamaica, lined with all types of businesses. At top, an image of Fulton Street from c1905 and at bottom, Jamaica Avenue in 2022.

Two vintage birds eye views of Jamaica in the early years of the twentieth century. At top, a view looking east on Fulton Street (later Jamaica Avenue), and at bottom, looking north toward a residential neighborhood in Jamaica.

Hardenbrook Avenue.   Jamaica, N. Y.

A turn-of-the-twentieth-century image of what is now 163rd Street in Jamaica (formerly Hardenbrook Avenue) shows attractive homes on a tree-lined street. There are still plenty of vintage late nineteenth and early twentieth century homes in Jamaica (along with some much more recent ones), as seen below on 88th Avenue in a 2022 photograph.

QUEENS GENERAL HOSPITAL, JAMAICA, N. Y.

7A-H432

Located at 164th Street in Jamaica just off the Grand Central Parkway, the Queens Hospital Center originally opened in 1935. The original main building was an eleven-story Art Deco structure of orange-colored brick, seen above in a c1940s image. Only one of the eleven original hospital campus buildings still stands. The hospital's current iteration encompasses 360,000 square feet with 200 inpatient beds.

8A-H1148

The Queens Supreme Courthouse building (aka General Court House) at 88-11 Sutphin Boulevard in Jamaica was built in 1936. It has a limestone façade and a Corinthian colonnade at the entrance. The image at top dates to the early 1940s. At bottom, the colorful twelve-story Joseph P. Addabbo Federal Building (used primarily by the Social Security Administration) at Parsons Boulevard and Archer Avenue in Jamaica was completed in 1989. The building's construction was marked by delays and major cost overruns; it was the subject of a federal investigation in 1988.

Jamaica High School was founded in 1892, and in 1897 moved into the Dutch Revival style building seen above in a c1907 image (the building is a NYC landmark and still stands). Outgrowing that building, it moved into its new home in 1927 (seen below in 2022), the massive Georgian Revival-style Jamaica High School building on Gothic Drive near Hillside Avenue in Jamaica Hills. It was once the largest high school in the country, holding up to 3,400 students. Crime and a declining academic reputation led to the school's closure in 2014 and its splitting into four separate schools on the same property.

CHAPIN HOME, JAMAICA, N.Y.

The Chapin Home for the Aging has a long history. Located on Chapin Parkway at 165th Street, north of Hillside Avenue, the home was founded in Manhattan in 1869 by Hannah Chapin (wife of Edwin Chapin, a noted orator and pastor), and has been in Jamaica Hills since 1910. As of 2022, it was a 220-bed nursing facility. The back of the c1910 postcard at top says "Dear Miss Washburn, The Flushing car at the bridge East 60th Street will transfer to Jamaica Car and this will stop at the house, it takes about an hour from the bridge. Hoping to see you."

Queens is home to several colleges, including the very popular St. John's University in Jamaica. At top, three St. John's professors during a strike at St. John's University in 1966, conferring at strike headquarters: (left to right) Ken Lazara (physics), Dr. Carlo Prisco (modern languages), and Joseph V. Phillips (fine arts; strike chairman). At bottom, a graduation ceremony for the class of 2021 was held in July instead of May due to the Covid-19 pandemic.

The Jamaica Soldiers Monument, currently located in Major Mark Park (named after World War I hero John Mark) at 173rd Street and Hillside Avenue, was designed in 1895 and moved to its current location in 1960. A depiction of Victory alighting from her clouds was chosen as it was decided that there was no way to make a soldier in uniform aesthetically pleasing.

Eastwood, Jamaica, L. I.

The Jamaica Estates development was one of several planned communities in Queens. Built in the early twentieth century on about 500 acres between the Grand Central Parkway and Hillside Avenue, the community was designed in English architectural styles, with a heavy focus on Tudors. This neighborhood was where Donald Trump spent his childhood. At top, the "Eastwood Gate" to Jamaica Estates c1915, and at bottom, the Midland Parkway entrance in 2022.

In the 1920s and 30s, Fresh Meadows was known for the 141-acre Fresh Meadows Country Club, which saw the likes of Babe Ruth and Babe Didrickson in a 1937 charity event. The property was purchased by the New York Life Insurance Company in 1946 and developed into a massive residential complex with numerous two- and three-story buildings that could house a total of 11,000 residents. The development included a shopping center, theater, nursery, and bowling center. Since then, the property's ownership has changed hands several times.

A commemorative cannon sits on the PS 35 Nathaniel Woodhull school property (90th Avenue and 191st Street) in honor of the martyred General Nathaniel Woodhull, who was fatally wounded by British soldiers at a tavern (torn down over 100 years ago) a few blocks northeast of that spot in 1776 as British forces swept through and took over Queens. The cannon was placed in 1904, on the twentieth anniversary of Founder's Day in Hollis. At top, a c1906 photo of the cannon, and at bottom, as it appeared in 2017. Inset, the actual spot of the tavern where Woodhull was attacked is now apartments.

A postcard advertising the Queens County Catholic War Veterans Model Home of 1955 at 192nd Street and Hillside Avenue in Hollis, and the area as it appeared in 2022. The full development of eastern Queens suburbs generally happened later than those in western Queens.

The Independent Order of Odd Fellows built a home on an eleven-acre property in Hollis in 1892. Located at 194-10 109th Road, the home was intended as a residence for elderly Odd Fellows, and their wives and/or widows. On dedication day in June 1892, a crowd of 5,000 people was gathered. The home was eighteen rooms (with an addition added later). The property featured a windmill with two 4,000-gallon tanks to supply the home's water. As of 1900, there were seventeen residents of the home—fifteen men and two women. There are no traces of the home left today.

St. Gabriel's Episcopal Church in Hollis is located at 196-12 Jamaica Ave (196th Street). It was established in 1887, when Hollis was a small and recently founded community. Services were originally conducted in the Hollis schoolhouse and moved into a permanent home in 1891. That church building, seen in the image above, was demolished in 1959 and replaced with the current structure, seen below.

Holliswood Hall was a spectacular mansion built in 1904 at 197th Street and Dunton Avenue in Hollis, north of Hillside Avenue. With forty-four rooms and eighteen baths, the building sat on ten acres of landscaped woodland. Built by art collector Samuel Shaw, it cost about $120,000 to construct, and a 1918 addition was an additional $70,000. The mansion did not last long; it fell victim to the demand for residential development and was purchased and razed in 1938. The Holliswood apartment complex occupies its former site. The image at top dates to about 1917.

The Belmont Motel Inn on Hempstead Avenue (Route 24) in Queens Village is located near Belmont Park (and now the UBS Arena as well). The *c*1960s postcard at top advertises the "luxurious accommodations" and touts it as fully air-conditioned with free television in every room, and a phone in every room as well.

The Little Sisters of the Poor Queen of Peace Residence, located on 221st Street in Queens Village, was founded in 1970. The vintage 1970s image at top shows residents in the garden of the facility. At bottom, the St. Ann's Novitiate, a convent that is at the front of the Queens Village complex at 110-39 Springfield Boulevard, seen in 2022.

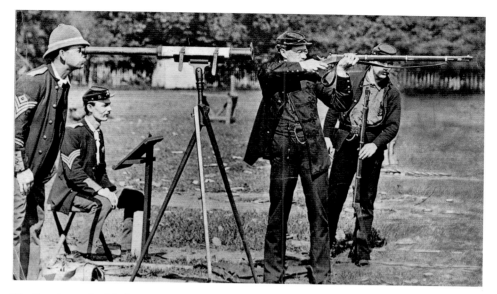

The Creedmoor Park Rifle Range opened on a flat expanse of land in what is now Queens Village in 1873. It was owned by New York State and hosted many shooting competitions. The range closed in the early twentieth century and was replaced by the Creedmoor Psychiatric Center, the campus of which is now largely comprised of abandoned buildings. At top, an 1880s print showing the Creedmoor Range. At bottom, the Creedmoor Psychiatric campus with main entrance off Winchester Boulevard (center of the image) as seen in a 2002 aerial view. To the northwest is Alley Pond Park.

The Creedmoor Psychiatric Center is like a time machine, with several of its buildings frozen in the moment they were abandoned. At top is one of the buildings on the old Creedmoor campus in 1993. At bottom, an abandoned Creedmoor building in 2015.

MOST ELABORATE IMPROVEMENTS OF ANY LONG ISLAND SUBURB

ONE OF THE BEAUTIFUL HOMES AT LAURELTON

With the incorporation of Queens into New York City in 1898, development sped up in many places. Laurelton, in southern Queens, is one example. A c1905 image of Laurelton, south of Jamaica, reads "most elaborate improvements of any Long Island suburb." Once Queens became part of New York City, Queens developers raced to build neighborhoods and attract homebuyers. At bottom, a 1920s image of a woman in front of a recently built home in Laurelton.

One of the oldest buildings in Queens sits near the water in the northeast corner of the borough. Built in 1819 by Wynant Van Zandt, this cube-shaped building in Douglaston was bought by George Douglas in 1835. The manor house originally sat on 175 acres of property, which was sold off in 1906 and developed. The homes currently on the former Van Zandt property are all part of the Douglas Manor community, a New York City historic district. The building's third story was added later when the building became a clubhouse. At top, as the Douglas Manor Inn *circa* 1910s, and at bottom as the Douglaston Club in 2017.

Bellerose is another Queens community that exists in both a Nassau County and a Queens County version. The section adjacent to the Bellerose LIRR station is known as Bellerose Village (Nassau), while the section just west of that is Bellerose Terrace (Nassau). The area on the north side of Jericho Turnpike is Bellerose or Bellerose Manor (Queens). In the top image, a view of 252nd Street north from Union Turnpike in 1950. At bottom, looking east on Jamaica Avenue (Route 25) in Bellerose, 2022. The left side of the street is Queens, and the right side is Nassau County.

LAWN AND PRIVATE CONSERVATORIES OF
JOHN LEWIS CHILDS, FLORAL PARK, N. Y.

Floral Park's origins date back to the late nineteenth century and the thriving seed business of John Lewis Childs (1856-1921), who started the first seed mail order catalog in the country. Like its neighbor Bellerose, Floral Park is a community that was split when Nassau County was formed. In 1899, southern Floral Park became part of Nassau County and northern Floral Park remained in Queens and hence was part of New York City. At top, the home, lawn, and private conservatory of Childs in what would become the Nassau County part of Floral Park once the split occurred. At bottom, looking north on 256th Street in Floral Park, Queens, north of Jericho Turnpike, just past the county line.

Post Office Building — Forest Hills, Long Island

Queens is home to numerous Art Deco beauties. The Forest Hills post office, located on Queens Boulevard at 70th Avenue, is one of these outstanding relics. Built in 1937 and designed by Lorimer Rich (and seen above in a 1940s image and below in 2022), it still stands today. The building features a beautiful relief sculpture, among other flourishes.